THIS REPORT IS STRICTLY CONFIDENTIAL

Dagger Editions, an imprint of Caitlin Press Inc.
3375 Ponderosa Way
Qualicum Beach, BC V9K 2J8
www.daggereditions.com

Text design by Vici Johnstone
Cover design by Shannon Olliffe
Printed in Canada

Caitlin Press Inc. acknowledges financial support from the Government of Canada and the Canada Council for the Arts, and the Province of British Columbia through the British Columbia Arts Council and the Book Publisher's Tax Credit.

Canada Council for the Arts   Conseil des Arts du Canada   BRITISH COLUMBIA ARTS COUNCIL   Funded by the Government of Canada   Canada

This report is strictly confidential / Elizabeth Ruth.
Ruth, Elizabeth, author.
Canadiana 20240357329 | ISBN 9781773861425 (softcover)
LCGFT: Autobiographical poetry. | LCGFT: Poetry.
LCC PS8585.U847 T45 2024 | DDC C811/.6—dc23

THIS REPORT IS STRICTLY CONFIDENTIAL

Elizabeth Ruth

Dagger Editions 2024

OTHER BOOKS BY ELIZABETH RUTH

Ten Good Seconds of Silence (Dundurn Press, 2001)

"Elizabeth Ruth's prose bursts with colour and metaphor. Clever and compelling, her debut novel is a dramatic portrayal of the inter-generational tensions surrounding memory, perception and identity." Camilla Gibb

"Elizabeth Ruth's first novel reveals a highly creative writer who is not afraid of taking risks. She finds her imagery deep within her characters, with the kind of innovative storytelling that is binding new readers to new writers." Timothy Findley

Smoke (Penguin Canada, 2005)

"Ruth is an innovative storyteller.... so full of vitality, so drawn to so many things simultaneously, so alive, reading her is always likely to be more of a D.H. Lawrence roller-coaster than a Virginia Woolf Ferris wheel. Ruth is utterly compelling." T.F. Rigelhof, *The Globe and Mail*

"*Smoke* is astute, big-hearted, occasionally disturbing and—as the title would suggest—nothing short of smouldering." Robert Hough

Matadora (Cormorant Books, 2013)

"With intelligence as well as passion, *Matadora* asks what it would have taken for a Spanish woman in the 1930s to walk into the bullring, staking her life on that peculiar ritual. Elizabeth Ruth's novel, testing the limits of commitment (artistic, literary, political and erotic) in the midst of bloodshed, is as magnetic and powerfully uncompromising as its heroine." Emma Donoghue

"*Matadora* is a character-driven novel and Luna must be counted among the most vital and alluring of Canada's literary heroines. She simply enthralls." Donna Bailey Nurse, *The National Post*

Semi-Detached (Cormorant Books, 2023)

"Part love story, part ghost story, part murder mystery—Elizabeth Ruth's *Semi-Detached* is all heart. Fiercely compelling and beautifully nuanced. A modern novel for the ages. Just brilliant." Helen Humphreys

"*Semi-Detached* will cast a spell over you. Elizabeth Ruth has crafted a beautiful and tender tale of shelters we all need to house our love and our yearning." Lynne Kutsukake

Love You to Death (Grass Roots Press/Good Reads Series, 2013)
A plain language novella for adult literacy learners.

Bent on Writing: contemporary queer tales (Canadian Scholars Press/Women's Press, 2005) An anthology.

Barbara Gail Pettigrew on her fiftieth birthday.

Dedicated to the memory of my aunt, Barbara Gail Pettigrew (a.k.a. Babs)—
thirty years in the institution, a lifetime trying to be herself.

Contents

Ward of the Crown

Love Child

Everyone Placing Bets

High Gloss Girl

i carry your heart with me(i carry it in
my heart)i am never without it(anywhere
i go you go,my dear;

e.e. cummings

Ward of the Crown

WARD OF THE CROWN

Forget diamonds and rubies, give me the bloodless
saphiret and peacock eyeglass, French-sounding
cabochon sweet bullets, these are the gemstones
without suffering, I am a crown made of dragon's breath

saphiret and peacock eye glass, French-sounding
single drop of gold added to blue, vintage
without suffering, I am a crown made of dragon's breath,
not a ward of the crown but a heart-shaped Marner bead

single drop of gold added to blue, vintage
Swarovski made me a mid-century girl, breathing to simulate fire opal.
Not a ward of the crown but a heart-shaped Marner bead.
Schiaparelli's, signed Judy Lee's, marked DeLizza and Elster.

Swarovski made me a mid-century girl, breathing to simulate fire opal,
seed pearl, turquoise, I dress for coronation day.
Schiaparelli's, signed Judy Lee's, marked DeLizza & Elster,
iridescent with rhinestones, round cut and marquis, a purplish cast,

seed pearl, turquoise, I dress for coronation day,
stippled, clear Lucite, imperfect slabs. I am
iridescent with rhinestones, round cut and marquis, a purplish cast, royal,
not made for aircraft windshields or fine company.

My shape is set in precious metal, highly collectible but
seed pearl, turquoise, I dress for coronation day.
Drilled through the middle, coloured or clear, I am
iridescent with rhinestones, round cut and marquis, with a purplish cast. Royal.

THIS REPORT IS STRICTLY CONFIDENTIAL

Babbling, she receives a token
for appropriate behaviour. If noticed
babbling for more than ten seconds sit her in a therapeutic chair.
Time out. No horseback riding, no outings.
Send cash donation to upgrade wardrobe.

0700	2 mg Cogentin
0700	3 mg Haldol
0800	25 mg Largactil
1200	3 mg Haldol
1400	2 mg Cogentin
1400	3 mg Haldol
1400	Senokot tablet
1400	Milk of Magnesia 30 cc + Cascara 5 cc

She may exchange her token for a diabetic candy
or the right to call home. Must sweep ward dining room floor
unprompted, work full time in the Laundry Department.

Patient has severe constipation. Send cash.
Send cash to replace footwear.
Send cash to replace winter coat.
Trouble sleeping. Send cash.

Patient very drowsy, needed help to walk,
trying to talk to herself all day, discouraged,
finished meal crying, crying and wandering
in dayroom, asking to phone home, crying,
babbling incessantly, homesick babbling,
babbling getting worse.

Patient sleeping too much. Woke,
pacing and extremely loud, loud at intervals,
pacing and babbling in dayroom, colouring,
wandering ward talking quietly to self.
Trying to find her suitcase.

Drowsy, skin clammy, a little whiny at times,
singing, watching TV, refused breakfast,
asking to go home,
babbling crying, babbling
"I don't like it here."

IDIOMS

scarce as hen's teeth, you were where?
there, where they put you, right there.

There, where they put you
to lie through them, spy through them,

scarce double dare. You were there
and not there, where they put you

scared, teeth on edge. Right there
where they put you, not long in the tooth

but long in there where they put you
scarce as hen's teeth, you were where?

there, where they put you, right there.
pulling teeth where they put you, in there

where they put you, scarcely
in there, where they put you right.

TRANSLATION

Do trees talk
maybe, about moodiness

> *She can be a pleasant lady in peer program. At times,*
> *will do something nice.*

a honey locust monologue
knowing what it's like.

> *Could get into Hilltop with high functioning people*
> *like herself. Maybe her attitude, behaviour, whatever, will change.*

Do they confess to that gaping atmospheric wound we call sky?

> *She addressed Dr. Maloney as Dr. Baloney.*

Or, bother to engage the sun?
That gassy, hothead nurse dispensing vitamins.

> *Token for diabetic treats withheld.*

If you piss them off, the bigtooth aspen and slippery elm,
they get good and mouthy, and

> *Her behaviour is unacceptable.*
> *She must be asked a question three times.*

A snapped branch that knocks you to your knees.
The wet threat of a leaf on pavement.

> *When a response is given, it is with attitude (snotty).*

What language is this? Treelish? Surely
a sugar maple is telling you to fuck off.

She will yell back. On 2 occasions
has gotten up and walked out of group.

When she dares to drain of sap,
denying you. Sweetness.

MUSIC THERAPY WITH MIRNA D

9–9:30 a.m. Mondays

Remind Barbara about
how she looks. Encourage her
to *wop-bop-a-loom-a-boom* care for
her appearance. Also cosmetics
to help *boom bam* self-esteem.
Barbara, she knows just what to
do *tutti frutti* au rutti. Participate in
swimming, Ladies Club and ward classroom.
She rocks to the east. She rocks to the west.
She's the gal that I love best when she can
do rug hooking. Encourage visits
wop-bop-a-loom-a with boyfriend.
Boom-bam thank you Ma'am!
Tutti frutti, perhaps on Sunday
bop-a-loom afternoons.

COTTAGE LIFE

Looking for that dream cottage
you deserve?
a slice of heaven.

*One wash basin to serve 64
one bathtub for 144
three shower outlets and eight toilets.*

Helpless, many cannot be toilet trained.

Plan your visit. Come
see renovated heartbreak.

*It is, of course, no Belsen. In many respects
and they are coming in at a rate of three a day,
a retarded child,* a retarded child, a child.

*Even the new hospital school at Cedar Springs
cannot accommodate this number.* Just think,
year-round enjoyment

underneath those peeling wooden ceilings

or punishment in the pipe room

*the stench appalling, beds crammed
head-to-head, less than a foot apart.
90 in a room designed for 70*

*gaping holes in worn plaster, floors pitted,
patched with ply. Planks spread and split,
leaving gaps*

do not say that you did not know

what it was like, the crevices
that cannot be filled. Leaky roofs.
Move-in condition will always cost more than a fixer-upper.

They could erect new buildings,
tear the old ones down. But winterized cottages
command a higher price

and the waiting list

just too many knock, knock, *knocking.*
4,000 names on the file. People
in beds on the verandah.

Beds in classrooms,
in occupational therapy rooms
that can no longer be used for play.

It is distressing to visit.

The Asylum for Idiots.
The Ontario Hospital School.
Huronia Regional Centre.

Overcrowded and understaffed,
a patient suffocates to death
but do not blame the present

department of health. Planning is key!

You have been told,
work hard, save smart.

You'll get there, eventually.

Italicized lines attributed to Pierre Berton's exposé in the *Toronto Daily Star*, Jan 6, 1960. Reprinted in *The Toronto Star*, September 20, 2013.

PELVIC EXAMS

Trusting relationships remain
problematic. Use Jimmy
a social reinforcer. Transfer him over.
Transfer Jimmy, reinforce
a steady.

Use Depo-Provera
injections at monthly
Sterilization? Tubal ligation?
She will be fitted
with an I.U.D.

Small uterus. Rectum clean.
External genitalia normal, feminine
without discharge. Without discharge,
there is some question as to whether
patient engages in anal. Apparently she has

a Jimmy, a nightgown, a tight hymenal ring.
She will not allow the speculum. Again
refuses to shower, refuses
to Jimmy relationships

I am unable
I am unable to
I am unable to insert a single digit.

REGRET

I hate to tell you, but Édith Piaf
was mistaken. Regret nothing of nothing?
She never met you, apologista extraordinaire,
queen of the Canadian pastime.
If you'd only been sorry for your slow gait,
walking on the balls of your feet,
for babbling, bad teeth and large print
that didn't line up just so. For sugar highs,
OJ at midnight, for those Amelia Earhart arms
that wouldn't stay grounded at your sides.

If you'd only been sorry for gifting small packages—
ChapStick and tissue, for your stash of sugar-free candy
small pleasures hidden in your drawer,
and those two family photos, face down.
If only for needing help with the VCR,
eyeglass cleanser, navigating stairs.

If you'd been sorry for mealtime tiaras,
fightin' words and a laugh like an exploding piñata,
or wearing black and gold not pink and white,
a thirst for Diet Coke, fear of dogs and snakes,
and hating winter. If only for those things, nothing more—
then regret would merely be any entry
in the OED, an expression of sorrow
or distress, or polite apology, not this feeling
of living in a world less loved.

---

with a nod to Mary Ruefle's "Merengue"

SUGARING

We rotated the spile, avoided
damaged areas, did not drill
within six inches of a former tap.

Still sixty years of collecting
left no place unscarred.
Your pincushion fingertips, calloused hips.
The tender of your belly, toughened.
Rough dry thighs, buttock like bark.

Some see sap as a miracle
when excess water boils away.
You cried, wonders are only sweet
to those who don't bleed.

SANITY SONNET

Of rejection, maybe?
Normal is a neurotic fear;

a genetic stamp, approval. Or
an argument with nature.

Treatments have been developed
should you consent, you should

change your outlook,
your degree of control.

Drugs? ECT? Sugar-free candy?
In a society filled with madness

do you understand what I'm saying?
Sane people, sane people

sane people also insist
there is nothing wrong with them.

A SNAIL IS CLIMBING UP

A small thing, me, a small thing looking up
the length of you, Sweetgum, inch by inch
I ascend, one hundred feet to the top
trailing ink over grey bark, your paper skin,
the distance between what I once thought I knew of mercy

and what I can no longer forget. Trying
to make meaning, trying to tell you how

my radula, scraping lichen and memory,
I taste sugar blood, bitter liquid amber
every part of me a tongue.

Gumballs, what children call your fruit
shallow root, dense shade, *Liquidambar styraciflua.*

A tree keeps carbohydrates as food,
breathes in reverse, heartsick, stops.
Then what? Prayer? Heroics?

I crawl up into my shell, from my perch
the verdant veins of your star-shaped leaves,
five points like five fingers, pale as sap runs dry.
I hear the little clock inside my own chest
do not, do not, do not.

Resuscitating a tree takes great skill,
and the best measure is compassion.

BIG, BAD BEAUTIFUL BOOK OF WORDS AND A TREE

I arrive at the group home to pack your life and find her weeping,
fingering your trinkets, as though she's lost a sister,
the half dozen open jewellery boxes, each a placebo
against joylessness, gaudy gemstone rings
that slipped on easily, bangles managed with diabetic hands,
the kind of brooches found at yard sales and that children covet.

This one is young, maybe twenty-five,
thinks a college course in residential treatment entitles her,
a better saviour, she establishes a bond.
She thinks mahogany is hair colour
old ladies and madwomen wear,
maybe Motown her mother used to hum,
not a tropical tree of the genus Swietenia,
expensive as dried blood.

She slips your dictionary from your shelf, the one
I brought to your first institution, and her French
manicure puts me off. She dares to flip through
our pages, our words that we used
to build stories. Better than a trousseau
had you been permitted to marry, better
than all the fucking occupational therapy.

She looks puzzled. Didn't occur to her you could've been a reader,
or a willet with your own distinctive call. That you
knew the rivalry of siblings, how to cuss,
the company of those not paid to be with you.
Knew every Elvis song and how to grind
your hips to stir the naughty air.
She doubts it still; I can tell, as I stand in the doorway—
four banker's boxes, lids folded into bases, grief tucked.

A resident is just a fancy word for patient, a euphemism
for a nobody whose cadence falls below the barrier of sound.
Here, outside normal, the invisible discarded forgotten ones
cut to furniture, arranged along salmon-coloured hallways.
Swish-swish go the trees in paper slippers, one end to the other,
but she's the one weeping with all the pathos of a blank page.
I could kick her to her knees, Instead, I clear my throat,

take pity. Explain scarlet fever, sugar seizures, brain damage.
It's gonna be all right, honey, I say, consoling, slipping
our big bad beautiful book of words from her hands.
Let me help with that, my one arm
around her shoulder while she bobs,
salt-water tears staining my best blouse.

PANNING

Not a trace
beneath the midnight sun or
under my hand. Not a fleck

of Klondike inspiration.
I came to dig
because of him, the first

dusty, crusty whistleblower.
But a symbolic gesture
from a safe   distance

is a meaningless act
of commemoration

~

You were
nowhere, at first

so I dug and panned
until summer shouldered fall
and poured over

the hills like birch syrup.
You wouldn't like it here,
more dogs than people.

Malamute, Inuit sled dog
Samoyed, a Dawson mix and
the wolf, if you count her.

Where to put a life like yours?
Redacted, stacked in a box
under my desk.

Put you on this page
or in the dustbin? Forget you?
Impossible.

~

I see you everywhere now,
on the blank page,
in the white night sky, adrift.

Your majesty
pours from the confluence
of those two rivers.

Swift and swirl, I think.
Untold treasure
is not merely waiting underground,

a smart prospector knows
poems, like gold,
weigh more than water.

Love Child

DETROIT, 1972

Melted tar and river water, grease from GM. August
on the brownstone steps. Weed through open window,
radio blasts American Pie, Staple Singers *I'll take you
there*. Where cinders of riot smoulder, and everyone's a
draft dodger, hustler, groovy. The only white kid on the
block, accent a honky-tonk Canada goose. Mule drugs
in diapers across the border. Search for gutter coins.
Jump rope and mind the pink platform bell-bottom pimp
on the corner. Play air hockey in somebody's basement.
How to afford an uncertain future? Behind a Cadillac
Eldorado. Flip the gas cap, fit straws end-to-end, thread
down to siphon. Fill cheeks with the battery tang, don't
swallow. Spit into the bucket. Everything must go.

LOVE CHILD

1

Ira Hirsh FEINMAN, June 23, 1944–Nov. 27, 2015. In his 72nd year, his devoted wife at the mall, Ira shuffled away quietly, much as he had lived his life. Born in *love child* Ont., Ira moved to Toronto to study at the University of *love child, love child* in 1966. Educated first as a chemical engineer, later as a lawyer, Ira had two *never meant to be* lives. A fiercely private man, Ira hid the *born in poverty* he'd fathered while on smoke break during a 1967 transcendental meditation retreat in Redondo Beach, CA, taking the secret to his grave. The only child of the late Shlomo *diff'rent from the rest* Feinman and Sarah (née Bronfman) Feinman, Ira will be nearly missed by his wife, Sheila Goldberg, three children (Larry, Curly & Moe) sister-in-law Rose, brother-in-law Joel and his now adult *love child, love child,* Elizabeth Ruth. A memorial service will take place in the far stall of the men's washroom at the Superior Court of Justice, Family Division. BYOTP. 361 University Ave., Mon. Nov. 30 11:00 a.m.

BOGOTA, 1975

Purple jasmine, valley wind. Jump hot pavement at the university
step on a crack and I can go back in the shadow of a new bullring
step on a line and I will be nine. Sniff bowls of white powder, coca,
car exhaust. Duck hailstones big as tennis balls. Little earthquakes
rattling furniture, my insides. I inhale your wet emerald earth,
suck pomegranate seeds, ear of corn. Hear your fine accent rolling
gold in the museo. A machine gun on every corner losing faith,
Escobar the rising Lord, and Monserrate reclining like Botero's
smooth fat nudes pinned behind my eyes, the weight of you,
the weight of you descending.

LOVE CHILD

2

Ira FEINMAN, Oct. 13/44–
April 25/16. Ira died suddenly
of a *love child*, while on his
daily stroll through Toronto's
High Park. Otherwise in good
health, Ira had recently been
suffering chest pain for which
he was *never meant to be*. Ira
moved from *love child* to *love
child* to study at the Circus
Academy in 1966. Educated as
a chemical engineer and as
a *(scorned by) society*, Ira is
survived by former wives, Sadie
Feinman (née Brown) and
Maria Galanti, (a Chilean
immigrant he met cleaning his
office.) And by his sons, Now
and Then. A solitary man, Ira
was haunted by letters, e-mails
and voodoo dolls from an
illegitimate. Working abroad as
a patent *love child* Ira enjoyed a
life of *born in poverty* and often
returned home with bedbugs
and duty-free gifts. The 3rd child
of the late *diff'rent from the rest*
and Sarah Bronfman, Ira will be
missed by his *love child*, and
the neighbour who videotapes
him picking his nose in the
driveway. Burial will be the day
after tomorrow at sundown in

Northern Chile, in the Chuquicamata open pit copper mine of the Atacama Desert. Donations to the Canadian Heart & Stroke Foundation. Or, Crime Stoppers.

YEARBOOK

Interesting 4 years, eh? *Goodbye.* Well, you are so lucky your favourite flirt's going to U of T with you next year; remember 3X the # of parties. *Goodbye.* You're the sweetest even though you like dominant *Good bye*, we got a lot closer this year. Let's keep it like this. *Bye*, you're real good to talk to. *Au revoir.* Don't ever change. Good luck and all that other stuff. You've been the best friend I've never had! *Later gator.* PS I'm not giving *G'bye* your overalls back. *So long, farewell* don't think you can get rid of me. *Auf Wiedersehen* I'll be up every other weekend. *Sayonara baby!* If you feel crazy hold this mirror have an out-of-the-ordinary *Ciao, Adios.* It's not the end but a great new *parting is such sweet.* Don't ever forget me because I won't. *Toodle-do* Tom Petty Rules! *See ya!* You picked an inopportune time to have yours truly swan song The Book. *Peace out! Gotta fly* I'm intoxicated, y'know unable to operate heavy machinery like a pen or a spoon. *Pip pip.* On to be an "ARTISTE." *Bon Voyage!* In your ocean of friends count me as a . permanent w a v e *Goodbye.*

3

Ira Herschel FEINMAN, Feb. 9, 1944–Sept. 4, 2017. At the age of 73, in the arms of his (non-monogamous) partner of 35 years, Ira skipped away at the Toronto condo he shared with Lev Shulman, their Wheaten *love child* Butch, and cats, Marilyn and Celine. An advocate for LGBT rights, Ira was responsible for helping to *love child* the Rainbow Railroad, an underground *never meant to be* of support for fey and lock-lipped refugees fleeing *love child, love child* in their home countries. In 1966, Ira moved from The Big A-hole to *always second best* to study law and *love child* engineering. A proud outie, Ira was tickled purple and chartreuse to have been contacted by the daughter he'd unknowingly fathered before coming clean. The eldest of 5 *diff'rent from the rest* born to the late Asher and Mindy Klein, Ira leaves behind his partner, Lev, their besties (ex lovers) and his now *love child, love child* also of Toronto. Celebration of Life to take place at the next open mic night at

Pete's Candy Store in Brooklyn, NY. Giveaways to include Ira's prized collection of (1000 pieces) of Dubble Bubble Bubble Gum.

LET ME INTRODUCE MYSELF

Spine a nervous quiver, head a wick
igniting fire. This idea, that one
feeding flame. Blue green, I am
a mineral compound with iron properties.

Tourmaline guts, mind, will. My hands
are typewriters, with six qwerty fingers
that spell *shiksa*. A dangerous defendant,
mouth like a live birth or

a flesh-consuming plant. I am
that big discard, your jetsam
thrown over. With more spine than you,
a nervous quiver, head a wick
igniting ire. This idea, that one.

4

Ira H. FEINMAN, May 7, 1944–July 1, 2017. Passed in hospice after a lengthy battle with *always second best*. Born in *love child* and adopted as an infant by Yoeli and Dafna (née Katz) Feinman, an ill-suited couple with impossibly high expectations. Moved to Toronto to study at the University of *diff'rent from the rest*. Both a chemical *love child* and a sonofabitch, Ira battled addition and subtraction and ultimately wound up living between the sheets. A funny-looking man with an infectious *love child*, Ira guffawed easily and would have shat himself to know about the *never meant to be* he'd cryopreserved with an *estranged by society* in the industrial freezer at a Dairy Queen in 1967. Unfortunately, repeated attempts by his *diff'rent from the rest* to locate him failed. Many *born in poverty* in his Parkdale 'hood will remember Ira as the geezer who scribbled chalk prophesies and doomsday *love child, love child* on the sidewalk at the corner of King and Jameson.

Take a look at me will be missed by no one. Cremation has already taken place. To claim Ira's ashes contact the Office of the Public Guardian and Trustee. 880 Bay St. Toronto.

IN THE SHAPE OF A MAN

It always happens like this,
in the wee hours
when the world has gone to sleep
and I alone am left to sink
into the moonlight, as if
into a featherbed

with a hole on one side
in the shape of a man.

I don't think about you
by day. Never have.
In the light of the sun
no regret for what hasn't been.
No ache of nostalgia or

longing to fill an empty space.

In the nine-to-five
you simply, neatly, don't exist—
not real in any sense
that truly matters. But sometimes,
not often, if I've stayed up late
switched into the magic hour,

I find my fingers on the keyboard
searching out a snapshot
of you and your real children.

This is my private after-dark game and I play
assuming the puzzle without all its pieces
will never be solved.

Place head. Draw in arms, legs,
make an outline of a torso. Fragments
snippets and imagination.

What makes a father?
Who cares.
What makes a father?
Biology. No, not enough.
What makes a father?

~

My grandfather was a hard man. Or
a soft man who pretended
to be hard, like most.

Forty when I was born, a newly recovered
alcoholic with an acerbic tongue, gruff WASP
manner fuelled by haste and impatience,
no time for his eldest unmarried
who'd gotten herself pregnant. He'd never approved

of my mother's friends, Jews, Blacks, queers
and those not bound for jobs at the Bell Canada switchboard
or the Ford factory. People like her,
trying for a life they didn't believe
they had a right to deserve.

And yet, and yet,
from the moment he held me, I was his
and he was mine and there was not a
sliver of a second for the rest of his days
when that would not be true. My grandfather
was a hard man, but not to me:

This is how you peg bacon bits to the clothesline, feed the birds.
This is how you pick out a Christmas tree, string lights.
This is how to wind an electrical cord and not damage wires.
This is how you build a playhouse from refrigerator boxes, dress a turkey,
fix a pocket watch, rewire a lamp, refinish wood, use the instamatic. This is how
to bowl five-pin, ten-pin, fly a kite, cook smelts, popcorn the old-fashioned way,

parallel park, pack a truck like a pro. This is how you deal with men and boys,
who would take advantage. This is how
to be afraid and never let it show.

What makes a man
love a child as if she were his daughter?

BACKSTORY

with his lineman's pliers and screwdriver
he could fix anything
splice knob and tube using electrical tape
and a paper clip

rewire a lamp, one eye on the game
rig up the wall socket using a hairpin and tin foil
from a cigarette package

wiring must be the culprit, he'd say
if he could see me now, confined to this bed
I sleep on ice, wake in a puddle, the nerve still firing

electricity is a double L5 disc herniation
morphine can't touch, an ungrounded neuropathway
conducting from hip to toe

pass me them strippers, he'd say
stepping into rubber-soled boots. Ready,
grit your teeth, girl, then
he'd cut the current.

HYDROMORPHONE

Caused a traffic jam at No Frills today
can't keep up with the current at the check-out
a purple coin scarf around her hips, my eight-year-old
shimmies to *If you leave me!* Opens her arms wide, says c'mon
Mumma, dance me a traffic jam. C'mon, my girl pleads, says
I don't remember when you weren't like this. Down
another 3 mg today, gimpy-leg-broke-back-ugly-shoed-woman.
Not jamming on morphine at No Frills
her hips jangle, feet shuffle. A scene up the aisle
the sweats, a sloth's energy. I caused traffic
not frills. Checked out. Tucked Etta away
If you leave me! as the news went twitter twitter
about the blue jays. Bautista's flock.
They also failed to deliver.

BASTARD

1.

I'm the bastard, right? I'm the sonnofabitch for not opening your letters, for shredding and burying and burning them. Or, is it for not writing back? I write but don't send, see? I flushed one last year. Tore it to pieces in the handicapped bathroom at work. No one goes in there anyway, junkies shooting up and the occasional prostitute. Disabled lawyers don't exist except on Netflix, let's get real. I think your last one said something about you getting married or having had a baby. The letter, I mean. It might've been the one where you'd been accepted into a hospital study testing women with Ashkenazi backgrounds for the BRCA gene mutations. The only time you counted as a Jew, you wrote. You were disappointed when the test came back negative. I think you were trying to be funny. You've inherited my sense of humour?

2.

I suppose you think by now I would've told someone? My wife or the "re-wife" as Bernie calls her. One of my children? God, no. You become a certain somebody over time, the guy everyone depends on, who pays for drinks. The one the Rabbi calls that good-looking shmuck from Feinman, Goldfarb and Associates, the one who drives the 300 kilometers to Ann Arbor in a blizzard because his youngest broke her femur playing varsity volleyball (who knew that was even a thing?) and now she wants to quit her freshman year. You become that person to yourself, too, and maybe it's a little bit true and maybe you don't want to give that up. Because if you're not that guy then who the hell are you?

3.

I've noticed the postmarks. Always the last Friday of the month, like you're checking off that final item on your "to do" list. Friday January 31st: Find Father. Friday March 26th: write to father hoping he writes back. Friday May 12th: just a single line, a question because that's all there's time for, *who are you?* Then I guess you pop it in the mailbox and hope for the best. Well I'll tell you; by five on Fridays I'm at home watching Sadie light the Shabbat candles. Why do you keep at it? One letter each month since you turned sixteen. Jesus, that's a lot of landfill. Is it my punishment? An envelope as a small, neatly folded form of torture? When Lisa from reception brings the mail, she stops into Bernie's office before reaching mine, and I see it in her hand through the glass wall. A sick little missive, the white missile aimed right at me. I see it, like a peregrine falcon would see a mouse in a field and all I want to do is dive at her and destroy it before she can lay it across my desk.

4.

I'll admit it; if they stopped coming now I'd be nervous. Like regular heartbeats they are, or a form of echolocation?

A homing device, at least if I know where you are, I know where you're not; here, in my actual life, fucking it up.

5.

Bernie's retiring. 70 years young and he wants to read the paper in his underwear and not think about who deserves the carhousecottagesavings. He was going to wait but why wait, he says. He could drop any time. After all, his father only made it to 74. Where does that leave me? A name partner with no partner. It makes you think doesn't it? Times a tickin'. What if I kicked the bucket? Would you read the obit? Scoff at the things people had to say about me? What if you didn't know and the letters kept coming? Shit on a stick, Sadie would receive them. What if you showed up at my funeral? Jonah finding out he wasn't the oldest and Rachel not the only girl? What a scene! I'd almost want to be there.

6.

You'd be entitled to inherit.

7.

Jonah is leaving his wife for the shiksa. "Why be surprised?" Sadie said. "He's been sneaking around for years. And stop calling her that!"

"Just because he's a liar and a cheat doesn't mean he should be a shmuck," I said. I like his wife. She brings me soup to the office sometimes.

"Maybe if they'd been able to have children."

"I bet the shiksa can't cook," I said. Am I thinking what you're thinking; you're a shiksa too.

8.

I've never cheated. Thirty years as a divorce lawyer will curb the appeal. I'm just saying. Nobody's perfect but adultery isn't my failing. I'm guilty of ignoring the doctor's advice about my cholesterol, telling my kids the cat ran away when we'd had her put down, throwing out my dirty socks and underwear, instead of washing them when Sadie visits her sister, not caring enough in general. My sin is indifference. You know, your mother and I? It was maybe three dates. We made out in my car facing the Detroit river. You could smell dead fish and hops from the Hiram Walker. It was over in a flash and then I heard from mutual friends that she'd moved away. Go ahead, blame me. I can't argue the facts. We were twenty, it was the summer of love and, hell, I don't even remember her full name. Or her face. When I found out she was pregnant, I didn't want to press stop on my life. That's how I saw it then and that's pretty much how it's stayed. You weren't real to me, see? You were just this idea someone else had.

9.

So you're considering making a conversion? You're a weak hybrid and you want purebred status? Okay, that's not what you wrote. You wrote that the only things you'd ever known about me were that 1) I was a Jew, 2) I was a lawyer and 3) I had brown eyes, like you. That one you figured out on your own because everyone else in your family has blue or green or grey. Will you do it? Become a Jew? It's like a seesaw you say, belonging and not belonging? For a long time you didn't think you could claim the identity because it was mine and I wasn't your father. Not really. But now you've realized you don't need me to be who you already are. What a relief that is to hear. I am utterly unimportant, just as I'd always assumed.

10.

I went to Rabbi Zuntz and told him. Now what?

11.

Drive through take-out last night, sat in the empty parking lot, three cheeseburgers on my lap. Plural. Three of them, and a cardboard container of greasy fries. I could practically feel the fat clogging my arteries as I swallowed but could I stop? Not a chance. Something about that last letter. What does it mean, you sometimes feel invisible? If a tree falls but nobody wants to hear it, you said. You said, my silence is profound but it cannot erase who you are. Who are you?

12.

I had a client a few years ago, lost his job being chronically late to the office. The poor sap would get up, shower, dress like everyone else. Eat his oatmeal and be out the door. But, before he could get to the elevator and press the down button, he had to turn back, retrace his steps exactly, and check the door to make sure it was locked. Press repeat. He'd run through this same routine one hundred and fifty-nine times. One hundred and fifty-nine exactly (never asked why) and that would make him miss the bus, which in turn made him late for work. Every goddamned day. His wife eventually divorced him, that's where I came in. We settled fast, and he kept the condo but it wasn't much of a victory when you consider he's probably still there, OCDing, and missing out on a life.

TURNING FIFTY AT STEELES AND YONGE

Bring two stomachs she'd written on the invitation, an extra
pair of feet. The cover band will blast eighties power ballads
and klezmer.

She wore black velvet, arrogance
too often reserved for brides. And why not?
This was the wedding and the divorce

she never had, the bat mitzvah
too risky behind that iron curtain. Now
a fog of dry ice and a new course

served by Moldovans. Tiny pots of mushroom, cheese
chicken on swords, kefir crepes, tea cakes, too much red wine.

Round tables became fountains
of pickled herring, beet salad, cow's tongue.
Caviar spilled like tears.

We cheered—or was it jeered?—the drag queen in stilettos.
She did Tina then Michael then (yawn) Celine. The finale

a big-bottom, busty peasant stereotype
hava nagila hava nagila!

We roared at the in-joke
but when the waiters laughed too, I remembered
what it is to not belong.

You can't be a Jew and a Russian.
The paper from her exodus, a one-way ticket to stateless.
Reason For Departure stamped in black ink
a three-letter word.

Everyone Placing Bets

52 WEEKS IN A DECK
(LETTERS TO THE QUEEN OF HEARTS, 1994)

i

Finished washing the kitchen floor
with a mop. Babs, I do everything
the easiest way.

That's the deal now.

ii

for the chocolates and rose bush
also, thanks for coming and
celebrating Easter   rotation is clockwise

a week early.

iii

Great *Mamma Mammogram* Day
weekend. That was sure a hotel.

iv

This morning out to Woolco
two nice baby suits   heart and clubs   for Laura's shower
from you and me.

v

Yesterday the jokers and wild cards
came with their large truck,
washed the house and garage.
It took all day.

vi

Cousin Marie called. A blessing
Cindy died. She was only 44
but   chemo

Gloria has invited me to see acrobats.

vii

John is having a garage sale
all weekend. The stakes are high.
There seems to be no end to the junk.

viii

for coming home
for the letter, received yesterday,
for the phone call. It is always good
to hear from you.   I sometimes miss
doing antique shows, but

ix

Decided to go into Toronto. Ante up
3 good paintings to put *biopsy* into auction.
Be rid of them.

x

Just a few lines to say, "hi".
Am going to get my eyes checked at 11 a.m.
Now I'm drinking tea.

xi

Will try and phone in half an hour, hoping
I catch you right
            after snack and before naptime.

xii

Here I am, as promised. (Bluffing)

xiii

We have a very cool day here.
I bet   everything
you have a sweater on.

xiv

Thanksgiving will work out
fine   if we aren't together
we can have another little *malignant* phone visit.

xv

Was sure happy to see you. I'm sorry
you bumped your head getting out of the car.
Sometimes it feels like the deck is stacked, doesn't it?
Did you have a letter from me when you got back?

xvi

Now to our Christmas.

xvii

Feeling fine after having my lump
my lump removed. Just a bit sore.

Gloria took me   waited to bring me home.

xviii

When you come, soon,
I'll do something you like
better than turkey.

xix

Hope you and Dawn had—
I'm sure you would
a good visit.

xx

a small amount of snow last night.
Tomorrow the repairman from
Sears to *chemo* the washing machine
     –   no water will run in. So

xxi

One more week and
Here's an early letter before
we show our cards, pick you up.

xxii

I'll call on New Year's Day.

xxiii

Did you take your shoes off while riding back?
Hope so as it would rest your swollen toes.

xxiv

Heather got moved in *sore mouth* and is putting
hair loss things away.

Aunt Dorothy was visiting her sister
Remember when we first moved?
Heather used to babysit her oldest.

xxv

Happy New Year once again!
Beth and boyfriend, Dave, are
still sleeping. They overbid,
stayed in last night

didn't even visit any of Beth's friends.

xxvi

My check-up at clinic was fine.
I go again March 9, some tests
to find out

am still knitting on that bright
coloured sweater.

xxvii

Just finished my supper, turkey
pie again. I think
I'll have a shower.
To-morrow CAT scan.

Try not to be worrying.

xxviii

a thunderstorm at 4 a.m. Flourishing
grass where the garden used to be.

xxix

Glad I went to Beth's graduation   a big day
for her.

xxx

While Dawn was at work
Liz Martin came over   *loss of appetite*
and Rita Markham   *fatigue*   for a few hours.
So I got to visit with a couple of old friends.

Liz also came to the train   carried my bag.

xxxi

Our tulips are all out and
they look

xxxii

It was good talking last night
hope you can you can you *cancan*
stop worrying.

xxxiii

Mrs. Krech brought over a container
blueberries—picked them herself
            imagine, 80 ½ years old.
Wish I could follow suit.

xxxiv

My neighbour Kathy just
phoned to see how   I am.

xxxv

By the time you receive this
you will know

your shopping trip will have *metastasized*
a couple of weeks
but time will pass
            before you know it.

xxxvi

Well, the homemaker finished
at 12 o'clock. Back on Thursday.
This afternoon the VON.   I plan on just *stage 4*
getting up for pills and snacks.

xxxvii

all the little witches and goblins.
Mothers fixed up costumes
just like I used to do   for you.

xxxviii

Last night a big fat trick,
Heather and Bob phoned from their holiday
        I held my glass of water
up to my ear to talk. We thought
that was funny.

xxxix

_____

xl

Stephanie is writing this
so   groggy and hard to concentrate. I think
I even forgot to write to you last week.

xli

Heather has been here taking care of me.
Bob and Marion came, Joyce,
everyone placing bets.
Joyce baked cookies and oatmeal crisp.

Excuse the pencil again, but I guess
as long as it is a letter.

xlii

My last treatment is on Monday
unless

xliii

Heather is going home tonight.
We have a lady named Margaret *See you soon*
filling in for a while.

xliv

Called you a few minutes ago
a nice little visit. I hope

you can stop worrying about me so much.

xlv

Here I am again, already.

xlvi

John is putting a new   *liver*   light in the kitchen.
I wanted a change.

xlvii

a hospital bed in the living room.
a hospital   in the living room   a bed
in the hospital.

xlviii

Please   try to not be worrying too much.
Your sisters will help re-deal
get things arranged *get things arranged*
for you.

xlix

Guess what I just got in the mail? A basket full of beautiful.

l

a sponge bath
and sitting in a big lounge chair
out in the halls. This is the hand I've been dealt.

The nurses were busy all morning with Shirley,
put her on a rubber stretcher in a
rubber boat-like thing to shower her.
You take care, Precious

li

Ellen came in and brought me
paper and *I'll be thinking about you* envelopes.

lii

John has a fresh cold so he isn't coming
up today. It still looks to be frosty outside.
The days sure do seem   long.

Time to fold.

I get lots of *XOXOXO* weather reports.

High Gloss Girl

THE BASILICA

I wish I were a believer
in fast food, this cult of bread and wine.
Oh, to be comforted by the promise of saints,
bright hot offerings against despair, to believe
in absolution as Laval did,

Or that you can return to me, a resurrection
as shimmering and gilded. The wisp of time—
thirty years since we last sat here, together.

Our grandfather told me
God does not live in any house

If only I could climb the altar, toss a rope
over the angel's wing and draw myself
to Mary's high station. In your name, I would pull
Jesus down from his cross, pry the nails from his palms.
Forgive. Decades gone and still I haven't.

Doubts, I carry them
in the bloody pocket of my heart.

I spy the porcelain half-moon of holy water.
Dare to inch toward it, dip my fingers in.
I am eight years old again, passing for a Catholic,
taking the host on my tongue eagerly,
blaspheme, as I have taken women

and still, still I have not
saved anyone but my small self.

QUEBEC CITY PRAYER

Walking cobblestone streets, Sainte Anne to the boardwalk.
'Round the Chateau at sunset, green lights iridescent across the water.

Chunks of ice float down the river, dampness seeps all around.
Slight shift in perspective. I am dizzy from the flight or memory:

Ethan, my year of high boots and harmonicas
fucking in windows to Jacques Brel.

Dany was butter beef pot-roast, lessons in separatism,
his pants down around his ankles as he and my train pulled out.

Under the statue of Champlain I contemplate the Iroquois,
another dirty marriage proposal

my lover at twenty-two, high in a flat
with antique windowpanes, Neil Young

bleeding while that relationship fell with the rain.
This place warps time, bends it to a circle:

My sixteenth summer, you and I hummingbirds
hovering in the hotel lobby waiting for life to happen.

Well, life happened, fell hard like this stone underfoot.
We wasted ourselves banking on time, boys, a future.

Should've donned runners that night instead of eyeliner.
Should've fled toward risk and held tighter to each other.

Spring in Quebec City, a ruthless benediction
that snakes through winding streets bound for the St Lawrence.

I trudge uphill, two feet of melting, see the wall around the plain,
the moat that drops down to stone, disappointment.

A red barge slows through the narrows, cuts loose breakaway ice.
The maple leaf snaps atop the Dufferin lookout and there you are

at five, ruby jacket chasing along a boardwalk
at fifteen, carving poems into your arm like prayers.

I rush past a row of houses, stand feet from the monument to Wolfe
but the Governors' Garden does not interest me.

Only the river, chimera of change
and the blasting echo of your plea *don't forget me*

History will not remember your name or mine,
or a thousand other nobodies

with talent and ambition, not born with silver spoons,
right families, good timing.

Still I hear you in the thunder of distant
insurrections. Here, where the trickle and run-off sparkles

on pavement lit by the noon-day sun. I remember us
before the cannons were cold, before you disappeared

and I touched their iron bodies, then my forehead. This prayer
is a destruction too.

BALLOONS

fifty on my birthday, multi-coloured and fat
stored under your bed, invasive ductal carcinoma,
in black garbage bags, fifty adjectives written in marker
rebornfunartisticloyalmummabearrebelliousgiverof100%
each how you see me. Estrogen receptive, optimistic, HER2+
I am a lucky half-century, with half a pair. Floating down
to me at the bottom of the staircase

> hooters
>> melons
>>> boobs
>>>> knockers

balloons on my birthday. An interval
tumour with four loci and I am
rebelliousgiverof100%funloyalbearrebornartisticmumma
a mastectomy scar with creative cleavage, busty and brave.
In other words, tough tough titties.
In other words, still here.

EATING A PEAR WITH A KNIFE AND FORK

looks silly, doesn't it? Resourcefulness. The way
we adapt to circumstance. A knife to press though the thin green peel

when teeth are no longer an option. The fork to steady the fruit on the plate;
at least the hands still work. This is not how we once did things.

Anyone can bite into a pear, chew, swallow. Anyone
can lie flat at night and breathe.

Or wipe her own ass, for god's sake. People say
we are the unlucky. Dealt a raw deal.

It is true; fruit and vegetables pose a problem. The pear, especially
must be soft and juicy. Utensils found.

We learn to balance the immature hourglass on a plate. Time
spent sitting at table, wondering how to avoid hard produce.

Eating a pear with a knife and fork isn't that unusual. It's what you do,
what we all would do, saving our own lives.

A CLARET TRAIL

I walk on a sea of haemoglobin
bearing the mark of nailbeds
blackened, blood-soaked socks.

Monsters, what cancer makes of us, all
face sans eyebrows, lashes, sans breasts we are
hairless apes sounding a state of emergency

warning of a red and seeping
chemo crucifixion. Bad luck that might rub off
if not but for the grace of

there go I, drip, drip dripping plasma
a claret trail along the pavement, hardwood, the downward
spiral staircase. On my body identification,

tattoos of wild violets and cruor branding
me a 21st century stigmata. Bags of chemicals bubbling
into my veins.

A cure, a carmine stain
marking me, what is left of me
what is left?

US, IN THE KITCHEN AFTER CHEMO

twin teal goblets, leaning
into one another, hummingbirds
drinking the air

a pair of navy ankle boots, my boots-
with a square heel, laces and a fringe
my boots

without my feet

through the back window
a turquoise bicycle in the snow,
both wheels rusted

and in a tall glass vase
two midnight hydrangea
quivering

NGC 1052 DF2

The man with the handlebar moustache stands on a stepladder in the centre
of my dining room. Albert there, above the fray.

He holds the chain of the lamp, lifts one end of the link to
the ceiling while the glass body swings. Is this a good height?

Light should spread over us while we eat
but dark matter is everywhere, surrounds

like a halo throughout the universe. Dark matter
pulls normal matter to it. Mother hovers,

circling with a tea towel in hand, eager to dust
the brass patina of the frame, the lamp's body

which long ago held oil, and each marquise crystal
that will hook around the lip of the milk-glass globe.

She is afraid, speaking language meant to persuade, cajole,
me into doing this her way. Lower,

she barks. That's too high! We're not hicks
who hang their pictures far north. Poor Albert

still up there, arm trembling. That lamp is heavy,
irreplaceable. In the family four generations,

it dangled over my childhood like a reliable moon
in grandmother's butter yellow kitchen, in mother's on Bathurst.

Now it is mine. How much light is necessary for one
lifetime? How much is unbearable?

Albert clears his throat, impatient for an answer.
Lower? Higher? The lamp weighs. In his hand, 120 years

of oil-lit meals and incandescent bulbs. What if
dark matter is not inevitable. There's another ultra-diffuse galaxy

the size of the milky way? Could a mysterious,
invisible substance have its own separate existence?

It is possible. No dark matter
for new beginnings. Which will it be—

Tradition, fear unchallenged. Mismeasurement or
whole new worlds, as yet unseen?

GET WELL CARDS

Origin of a spiral, yup
it really sucks. The winding down
around fear—

I should know, right?
A tightening corkscrew
the C word, continuous and gradual.

In mathematics a curve,
in a watch the spring of time—
now, a gyre around which to twist

a proverb: No reason to fear the wind,
this earthly coiling, where
the root is deep.

~

Just keep
            swimming
blessing the boats
            with Lucille Clifton. Suffering
through this
            to that. The tide
that is *entering the lip*
            of your
understanding,
your eyes to water,
            and the rest
    sinking   sailing

~

July was Picasso's

A blue period, then
the iridescent seahorse. *Blue and green*
should never be seen. In autumn.

Dark green leafy laughs:
the next non-doctor
who thinks they can cure you
gets smothered with kale

and October poppies on recycled paper.

A November sunflower. *You are my*
sunshine, one chemo left
my only. The black poodle

of December. Shakespeare wrote

it is not the stars that hold
our destiny. *What now?*
but in ourselves.

~

the whole wide world awaits. Breathe

NOVA TOTIUS TERRARUM ORBIS GEOGRAPHICA

and don't forget that poison, poison
serves a protective function in nature.

~

high gloss girl in black and white

hanging laundry on a hill
in a grey way, wrestling
with the wall of wind,
each garment a year, a layer
of time clinging to bone.

This is how you do life:

peg each moment, balance
the basket between your knees
keeping on, one more sheet
one more robe, another minute
closer to the finish. And repeat

ON THE NINTH AVENUE TRAIL

Such a common tree gets little respect
for heartiness, overcoming

in lowland bogs and swamps. Or
high and dry, *Picea mariana* thrives,
her bristles stretched skyward—

courage, reaching
beyond suffering into uncertainty.

Across every province and territory
a simple conifer goes unrecognized
tolerating harsh environments

with bravura and backbone. Like us
here, in the aftermath.

You were nine when I found that lump.
I was 49, but a spruce doesn't count
time as horizontal. Instead, think ladders

living vertically, ascending like a thin pencil
writing into the future.

MORNING WALKS

The wooden steps of my front porch are rotting thin
oak leaves, a gentle brown net of fingers underfoot.
The geometry of primary colours at 1832 Gerrard, the artist painting
in a windy glass studio, how I am trying to outrun cancer,
how that is impossible.

Gerrard Street is an umbilical cord
connecting my house to my friend's, a lifeline in asphalt and concrete.

The 506 streetcar conductor wears his mask beneath his nose
and the old woman next door waves,
cuts her grass with scissors.
The last rose in bloom smells as it looks, bashful
and dewy, with a note of defiance.

The friend of a friend walking her silken-haired dachshunds
avoids my bald head. Pity
in faces of strangers because, missing eyebrows.

The sun streaming through a canopy of maples
in Monarch Park, three hawks nesting
potholes and cracked pavement   endless
home renovations, no one is satisfied.

How survival means creating the smallest life you can love—
my daughter, a bit of writing now and then, these walks.
How there are others careening between treatments
or dying, how everything is

dying, the last chrysanthemums, dehydrated cedars,
a squirrel flattened, raccoon run over at the light
and yet everything is born again:
tulips poking up through moist, dark earth
a robin's nest in the side of a brick wall,
the black-capped chickadees, the calendar
years, cycling back to beginnings—

September for schoolchildren, Sabbath re-sets
and me, post chemo.

How some of us are lucky, but not for long.
And some of us are lucky because we know that.
The sour cherry tree on Highfield in full fruit.
The taste of my neighbours' divorce. He leaves
with clothes and a car, and a much younger woman.

The drug dealer with his spiked mastiff.
The home daycare where everyone smokes.
COVID puppies, the anorexic who walks more than I do,
and in stilettoes, while reading the paper.

Pairs of middle-class mothers with blonde highlights and Lululemon.
The man on a tandem bike, his son with Down's Syndrome.
How white men rarely step aside when they see me coming,
and summer sun is a balm but only for twenty minutes,
then I am a sweaty peach.

A hydro pole wears a handknit sweater
and messages: *Hang in There!*
We're All In This Together! I Miss You!
How we're not all in this together, now or when it ends
only some of us will remain.

Certainty, how I miss you, too.

Black Lives Matter! Indigenous & Black Lives Matter!
We throw away valuables—planters, a desk, our lives,
can be indifferent to lawn furniture, a bread maker, each other.
George Floyd. Eric Garner. Thousands of children
found in unmarked graves at "schools."

Across this country we discard
imperfect toys, bicycles. Time.
Bricks and flagstone, vases, cups and saucers,

unopened office supplies, cat carriers, bird cages
but not the cages we have built for ourselves.
We put out baby gates, water glasses, a garden hose
a whiteboard with markers, hub caps, a bike helmet, all the detritus
from our outlived lives, our souls to the curb.

How tiny libraries punctuate Toronto
yet a library empty of patrons is a lonely, silent heart.
How people line up in a pandemic
for the food bank,
around the block for the liquor store.

Coffee Time is where poor men hang out,
middle graders rush Pizza Pizza.
Sunglasses are a must for the boardwalk at noon.
How you can make a new habit of movement, like a daily prayer.

No patrons inside the Islamic shop, ever.
How North Face is a marker of class, and we cross
the intersection while texting. The woman in flip flops
tells her best friend everything—a failing marriage
at full volume, a man chases up Woodfield after his toddler
learning to walk.

I am also learning.

For Sale signs don't last long (*Sold Over Asking!*)
Someone is living in the bus shelter, a doorway, the alley.
Encampments at Ashbridges Bay, everywhere—
safer sheltering outside during COVIDtimes.
Not enough beds anyway.

How seniors in long term-care are an afterthought, dispensable
like a wok at the side of the road, a black Singer sewing machine,
a ginger cat wearing a tiny silver bell and red collar.
We are living in a world less loved, skeletons

in purple and black robes dangling from trees on Halloween.
Thank You Front Line Workers but Fuck You, Ford!
How conservatives privatized healthcare and politicians
took lockdown vacations.

14 Pride flags in east-end windows, 71 drawings in crayon,
the sumac pointing north, soft optimism.
The pink-nosed, pink-tongued opossum, a coyote with mange,
a family of fox cubs, how family is everything
or nothing, without love.

Businesses boarded up in stage 3.
Stage 2 no longer exists
in a breast cancer diagnosis.
How daycare workers lead a rosary of tiny snowsuits
across the street, the Rabbi's family.
How my Rabbi just retired.

The sound of maple leaves crunching underfoot,
people raking make eye contact
after months of loneliness. Fall smells like warming spices.
The stroke victim two streets over is out too,
dragging his body through every kind of weather,
half of who he was to the grocer, pharmacy,
to take in holiday windows. We are all eager for light

Christmas bulbs and the odd Hanukkiah.
People keep their decorations up longer—
severed limbs and black cats and witches' hats.
How Georgia flipped a Fascist in November
and a racist nation still prefers its democracy to its dictator

but not really, and how we are no better.
We tolerate by degree, lobsters now in gradually heating water:
community spread, percentage positivity. The schools are safe, they say
while children sit home staring into the blue light of screens.

Canada Post and UPS play Santa, Amazon becomes the Prime ecology
not a rain forest. My neighbourhood
with porch pirates and grocery delivery. Saturday evening cover bands
on the corner of Woodfield and Fairford.

How the woman a few homes down steals our flowers after dark,
and the man with edema (diabetes?) limps his Borzoi every morning.
He used to head out for a dog park farther east, I would see him
before COVID, before cancer, by the tennis courts.
A little wind keeps the game interesting, breath is victory
and the mezuzahs in doorways, good company.

NOTES

The title of this collection is taken from the stamp printed across my aunt's official records from the institution in which she lived for thirty years. I obtained these records with permission, prior to her death.

The epigraph is taken from "[i carry your heart with me(i carry it in]" from *E.E. Cummings: Complete Poems, 1904–1962*, edited by George J. Firmage (Liveright, 2016).

THIS REPORT IS STRICTLY CONFIDENTIAL – a found poem.

WARD OF THE CROWN – a pantoum.

My aunt, a crown ward, was ironically a life-long collector of vintage crown brooches. Like people with disabilities, costume jewellery and semi-precious stones are often seen as less valuable than so-called "precious" gems or "able bodied" people. This poem insists on equivalency and equality.

In addition to her crown brooch collection, my aunt wore tiaras to supper. She liked to think of herself as a queen, not as a patient. This poem seeks to give her agency and reframe the legal designation that defined her life, thereby turning something ugly into something meaningful. I have also honoured this part of her in the form of a character named Mrs. Moffat, in my first novel, *Ten Good Seconds of Silence*.

A Crown Ward is a legal term for a minor or incapacitated adult placed under the protection of a legal guardian or government entity, such as a court. In past decades in Canada, to access social supports, many parents were required to relinquish parental rights, making their disabled family members wards of the crown. Once made a ward, a family no longer had decision-making power over their loved one's care, nor could they remove that person from care. This is what happened to my aunt, a misdiagnosed autistic child and type 1 diabetic.

In the 1980s, many government-run hospital institutions in Ontario were closed without a plan for housing residents or for continuing care. Hundreds of disabled adults were released from residential hospitals with no place to go, no life skills and no families. Many ended up on the streets. Because she had an older sister who advocated for her, Barbara was accepted into a Muki Baum Association group home in Toronto. There, she spent the final eighteen years of her life among autistic peers, in a home setting, with a private room, access to appropriate therapies, a day job, social activities and greater freedom than she'd ever known.

In 2013, a $35-million class action lawsuit was settled between former residents & survivors of Huronia and the Ontario government. At that time, Ontario Premier Kathleen Wynne formally apologized in the legislature for the government's role in failing to protect vulnerable residents from the horrific abuses and neglect they suffered between 1876–2009.

Saphiret glass was made in Gablonz, Czechoslovakia, in the mid-nineteenth century (now Jablonec nad Nisou, Czech Republic) by mixing melted gold into sapphire-coloured glass.

Peacock Eye Glass refers to a rare antique Bohemian lampwork foil glass made to resemble the eye of the peacock feather.

Cabochon refers to a gemstone that has been shaped and polished, not faceted. Cabochon was the default method of preparing gemstones before gemstone cutting was developed.

Dragon's Breath Opal is not opal. It has an opalescent sheen but is made entirely of glass.

Marner bead refers to Julio Marsella Marner's Rhode Island costume jewellery. The company was founded in 1946.

Swarovski is an Austrian jewellery brand launched by Daniel Swarovski in 1895.

Elsa Schiaparelli's avant-garde jewellery designs were some of the most sought after and collectible costume jewellery pieces of the twentieth century.

In 1947, William DeLizza and Harold Elster founded DeLizza & Elster, (D&E) in New York City. They designed and manufactured costume jewellery and accessories.

In 1949, Blanche Viano opened a small jewellery company, Judy Lee's, in Chicago. Popular in the 1950s and 1970s, Judy Lee's were mostly made in Victorian floral motifs using sparkling rock crystal and artificial pearls.

Lucite is a high quality, trademarked version of acrylic resin developed by DuPont in 1937. It was used during the '40s and '50s to make costume jewellery, and during wartime for aircraft windshields. Lucite is known for its strength and durability.

TRANSLATION – a semi-found poem.

COTTAGE LIFE – a semi-found poem that incorporates lines from Pierre Berton's exposé of Huronia in the *Toronto Daily Star*, January 6, 1960. (Reprinted in *The Toronto Star*, September 20, 2013.) Huronia is the "sister institution" of Cedar Springs where my aunt lived. Cedar Springs opened in 1961 and closed 2008. Population 937. My aunt lived in Fairview "cottage." Berton's article can be found in full on page 89–91.

PELVIC EXAMS – a found poem.

A SNAIL IS CLIMBING UP

"A snail is climbing up" is a line borrowed from "For a Five-Year-Old" by Fleur Adcock.

"Trying to tell you how" is borrowed from "When We Dead Awaken" by Adrienne Rich.

"Resuscitating a tree takes great skill" is borrowed from "Twenty-Seven" in *Ocean* by Sue Goyette.

52 WEEKS IN A DECK (Letters to the Queen of Hearts, 1994) – a semi found poem using weekly letters my grandmother wrote to my aunt in the institution, during my grandmother's final year of life.

NGC 1052 DF2 refers to an ultra diffuse galaxy in the constellation Cetus, which was identified in a wide-field imaging survey of the NGC 1052 group by the Dragonfly Telephoto Array. It has been proposed that the galaxy contains little or no dark matter, the first such discovery.

GET WELL CARDS references Henricus Hondius' decorative world map, first issued in the 1630 edition of the Mercator-Hondius Atlas. It is a famous example of baroque-style Dutch cartography. The images and sentiments in this poem were taken from cards sent to me.

LOVE CHILD – this suite of poems uses lyrics from a Motown song of the same name, made famous by Diana Ross and the Supremes in 1968, the year this author was born to an unmarried mother. The song is about bearing a child out of wedlock and the stigma placed upon mother and child that once accompanied the experience. My poem playfully interrogates the absent father.

YEARBOOK – a semi-found poem that uses messages from my high school yearbook.

Pierre Berton's exposé of Huronia in the *Toronto Daily Star*, January 6, 1960. Reprinted in *The Toronto Star*, September 20, 2013:

On the last afternoon of 1959, I drove to Orillia with a friend of mine and his 12-year-old son. The boy is handsome, with large, dark eyes, but he is not very communicative for he will always have the mind of a child. He is retarded mentally. On holidays he comes home to his parents. The rest of the time he is a patient at the Ontario Hospital school.

There are 2,807 others like him, jammed together in facilities which would be heavily taxed if 1,000 patients were removed. More than 900 of them are hived in 70-year-old buildings. There is nowhere else for them to go.

It is distressing to visit these older buildings, as I did last week. The thought of fire makes the hair rise on your neck. The stairways have been fireproofed; nothing else. The paint peels in great curling patches from the wooden ceilings and doors. Gaping holes in the worn plaster walls show the lath behind. The roofs leak. The floors are pitted with holes and patched with ply. The planks have spread and split, leaving gaps and crevices that cannot be filled.

The beds are crammed together, head to head, sometimes less than a foot apart. I counted 90 in a room designed for 70. There are beds on the veranda. There are beds in classrooms. There are beds in the occupational therapy rooms and in the playrooms that can no longer be used for play. On some floors the patients have nowhere to go except out into the corridors.

The stench here is appalling, even in winter. Many patients are so helpless they cannot be toilet trained. The floors are scrubbed as often as three times a day by an overworked staff but, since they are wooden and absorbent, no amount of cleansing will remove the odors of 70 years.

On one floor there is one wash basin to serve 64 persons. On another floor, where the patients sometimes must be bathed twice or three times a day, there is one bathtub for 144 persons — together with three shower outlets and eight toilets. Prisoners in reformatories have better facilities.

Designed for the wrong patients

The newer "cottages," as they are euphemistically called, are often excellently
designed, clean and fireproof — but they, too, are overtaxed and often
misused. Buildings built in 1932 for 144 patients now house 220. And
because they have been fireproofed, they now have the wrong patients in
them. They were designed to serve high-grade patients — those with an I.Q.
of 50 or more. But, because of the threat of fire, the more helpless inmates
have had to be placed in them. Those of higher intelligence have been
switched to the non-fireproof buildings because they are better able to escape
on their own.

The authorities face a serious dilemma at Orillia. In order to fireproof the old
buildings they would have to evacuate all the patients. But there is nowhere
to move them. They *could*, of course, erect new buildings, then tear the old
ones down. But the waiting list for the hospital school is so large nobody
really believes they could be torn down — even if others were built. There
are just too many people knocking on the door.

There are 4,000 names on the file at Orillia — names of people who have
applied to enter a retarded child in the institution. The active waiting list — of
people who have written within the last year — is 1,500. Even the new hospital
school being completed at Cedar Springs cannot accommodate this number.

In 1949, Orillia admitted 196 new patients. In 1959, the number had grown
to 310. At the present time they are coming in at the rate of three a day. The
hospital loses, by death or discharge, less than half the number it admits
annually. And so the terrifying problem builds up year by year.

There are several reasons for this. One, obviously, is the population increase:
for every 200 children born this year in Ontario, three will need institutional
care. Ironically, too, medical advances have almost doubled the lives of many
mentally retarded patients. The big move to the cities has made it difficult to
care for a retarded child at home, and the "village idiot" of our forefather's
day is likely to be a patient at Orillia now. Finally, because of a change in
public attitudes, people seek out institutions which they once shunned.

A patient suffocates to death.

Orillia is overcrowded and understaffed. These two evils recently produced a chain reaction that caused a patient's death. Three years ago there was a bad fire in the basement of one of the older buildings. The danger was so great that a supervising nurse from the neighboring infirmary was called to help evacuate the inmates. All were saved but, in the nurse's absence, an infirmary patient released a cloud of steam which caused one woman to suffocate.

Political considerations have made Orillia's situation more acute. The hospital was originally designed for children of six years and older. It is now heavily overcrowded with children under that age. Medical authorities are convinced that many of these would be better off at home during the early years. But many have by-passed the waiting list and the regulations because of pressure from Ontario MPP's.

Construction and renovation at Orillia comes under the Department of Public Works, long the focus for political patronage in Ontario. Until recently, the department has had little liaison with the Department of Health which operates the hospital schools. Instead of rebuilding from the ground up, to careful plans, it prefers to work in a piecemeal manner — patching and renovating. Often the pace seems maddeningly slow. The remodelling of the administration building at the hospital began last April. It's still not complete. By contrast, a private contractor completed the floor-to-ceiling remodelling of the Orillia YMCA, a $250,000 job, in just four months.

But Orillia's real problem is one of public neglect. It is easier to appropriate funds for spectacular public projects such as highways and airports than for living space for tiny tots with clouded minds. Do not blame the present Department of Health for Orillia's condition. Blame yourself.

Remember this: After Hitler fell, and the horrors of the slave camps were exposed, many Germans excused themselves because they said they did not know what went on behind those walls; no one had told them. Well, you have been told about Orillia. It is, of course, no Belsen. In many respects it is an up-to-date institution with a dedicated staff fighting an uphill battle against despairing conditions. But should fire break out in one of those ancient buildings and dozens of small bodies be found next morning in the ashes, do not say that you did not know what it was like behind those plaster walls, or underneath those peeling wooden ceilings.

DEDICATIONS

COTTAGE LIFE is for Jennifer Morrow, sender of poems.

BIG, BAD BEAUTIFUL BOOK OF WORDS AND A TREE is for L.D. Pettigrew

PANNING is for Dawson City friends.

YEARBOOK is for Windsor friends.

BACKSTORY is for Mick (Milton) Pettigrew.

HYDROMORPHONE is for Violet Pettigrew-Olliffe.

52 WEEKS IN A DECK (Letters to the Queen of Hearts, 1994) is for Mona Verna Pettigrew (née Armstrong).

QUEBEC CITY PRAYER is for Rebecca Chernecki.

BALLOONS is for Violet Pettigrew-Olliffe.

EATING A PEAR WITH A KNIFE AND FORK is for Bryan Young.

A CLARET TRAIL is for Brian Day.

US, IN THE KITCHEN AFTER CHEMO is for Shannon Olliffe.

NGC 1052 DF2 is for Suzanne Robertson.

GET WELL CARDS is for Sally Cooper, Pat Magosse, L.D. Pettigrew, Shelley Savor, Marcia Walker, Alissa York.

ON THE NINTH AVENUE TRAIL is for Violet Pettigrew-Olliffe.

MORNING WALKS is for Erin Rielly Clarke.

ACKNOWLEDGEMENTS

Thank you, Vici Johnstone, publisher & acquisitions editor of Caitlin Press, Sarah Corsie, editor & production manager, and Malaika Aleba, marketing & publicity wizard. I am eternally grateful for your enthusiasm in scooping up this collection and giving it a fantastic home within your Dagger imprint. Caitlin proves that small is mighty.

I gratefully acknowledge the team at the Writers' Trust of Canada for selecting me to be the Berton House Writer-in-Residence (2019) so that I could develop this collection. That time in Dawson City, Yukon, was invaluable. Some experiences come at the exact right moment. Thank you also to The Writers' Union of Canada for awarding a mentorship microgrant, which allowed me to benefit from the wisdom of poet Maureen Hynes, and to Maureen for her keen eye and ear. Thanks also to poet Brian Day, especially for lessons in the possibilities of punctuation, to Maria Meindl, who invited me years ago to read a couple of these poems-in-progress at her Draft series. To bill bissett for performing one of them, *Translations*, on stage with me. Thank you to Stuart Ross for the poetry Boot Camp and Sally Cooper for sharing the experience. I also thank Jennifer Angold Morrow, Sally Cooper, John Miller and Kathleen Olmstead for reading and commenting on these poems. Thanks also to writer Lee Gowan, coordinator at the school of continuing studies, University of Toronto, and to the university for employing me all these years. Thank you, Jeffrey Round, for first publishing my poems in *The Church-Wellesley Review* back in the '90s. And to the many shimmering Canadian poets working today, I cherish your words.

I thank the University of Guelph, Department of English and Theatre Studies for giving me the luxury of time to marinate in poetry. Shout-out to the 2015/16 MFA cohort. A special thank you to former program co-ordinator, Catherine Bush, to Hilary Rex and to Mahak Jain. Eternal gratitude to poets Dionne Brand and Kevin Connolly for putting up with my early attempts, and to Dionne Brand for suggesting that I needed to implicate myself more in the work. I gratefully recognize the Social Sciences and Humanities Research Council for supporting this work at that time.

Gratitude to Shannon Olliffe for designing a gorgeous book jacket for this collection and for decades of support while I write. And to our daughter, Violet, the best reason I know to keep doing it. As ever, a big thank you to Linda Dawn Pettigrew for the gift of a childhood that encouraged free thought and expression. I thank my late grandparents M & M, Denise Deziel, and all of my extended and chosen family. Thank you, friends old and new. You know who you are, and I treasure each of you. Life is only sweet with good company.

Above all, I wish to recognize my late aunt, Barbara Gail Pettigrew, whose thirty years in a government run residential hospital inspired this collection. Thank you for trusting me with your story. I miss you. None of these poems would exist if not for you. At long last, you have been immortalized as the queen you always wanted to be, and I always knew you were.

ABOUT THE AUTHOR

Elizabeth Ruth is the author of the novels *Semi-Detached*, *Matadora*, *Smoke* and *Ten Good Seconds of Silence*. Her work has been recognized by the Writers' Trust of Canada Fiction Prize, the City of Toronto Book Award, the Amazon.ca First Novel Award, and One Book One Community. CBC named her "One of the Ten Canadian Women Writers You Must Read." Ruth is also the author of a plain language novella for adult literacy learners entitled *Love You to Death*, and editor of the anthology *Bent on Writing: Contemporary Queer Tales*. She holds a BA in English Literature, an MA in Counselling Psychology, and an MFA in Creative Writing. Elizabeth Ruth teaches creative writing at the University of Toronto. *This Report Is Strictly Confidential* is her debut poetry collection.